VIETNAM

A TRUE BOOK®

by

Shirley Wimbish Gray

Children's Press®

A Division of Scholastic Inc.

New York Toronto London Auckland Sydney
Mexico City New Delhi Hong Kong
Danbury, Connecticut

A fishing village
in Vietnam

Content Consultant
Stephen M. Graw
Southeast Asia Program
Cornell University
Ithaca, NY

Reading Consultant
Nanci R. Vargus, Ed.D.
Assistant Professor
Literacy Education
University of Indianapolis
Indianapolis, IN

The photograph on the
cover shows a Vietnamese
girl by some bamboo plants.
The photograph on the title
page shows street vendors
in Ho Chi Minh City.

Library of Congress Cataloging-in-Publication Data

Gray, Shirley Wimbish
    Vietnam / by Shirley Wimbish Gray.
        p. cm. — (A true book)
    Includes bibliographical references and index.
    ISBN 0-516-24211-3 (lib. bdg.)   0-516-27774-X (pbk.)
    1. Vietnam—Juvenile literature. [II. Title. III. Series.]
DS556.3 .G73 2003
959.7—dc21   2002005899

1 2 3 4 5 6 7 8 9 10 R 12 11 10 09 08 07 06 05 04 03

Contents

CHINA

LAOS

Red River

Hanoi ✪

Gulf of Tonkin

VIETNAM

Mekong River

THAILAND

South China Sea

CAMBODIA

0   200 miles

0   300 kilometers

Ho Chi Minh City (Saigon)

N
W   E
S

Gulf of Thailand

VIETNAM

A Long and Narrow Country

Vietnam is a long and narrow country that is shaped like the letter "S." It is on the continent of Asia. A train ride from the southern end of Vietnam to the northern end takes about thirty-six hours. Vietnam shares its northern border with China.

To the west are Laos and Cambodia. Along its long eastern coast is the South China Sea. Many white, sandy beaches are found along the coast.

The capital city of Vietnam is Hanoi, which is in the northern part of the country. The largest city is Ho Chi Minh City, which used to be called Saigon. Hue and Da Nang are two important cities near the coast of Vietnam.

Two large rivers are located in Vietnam. In the north, the

Some citizens are standing outside City Hall in Hanoi (above). Crowds move through the streets of Ho Chi Minh City (below).

Red, or Hong, River flows from China into Vietnam. The Mekong River spreads through the south. Both of these big rivers branch out like fans into smaller rivers and streams. The rivers dump rich soil in the nearby flat lands, called **deltas**.

Mountains stretch through western Vietnam, near its border with Laos. Most people live near the flat coast. Few people live in the mountains.

Boats sail down a branch of the Mekong River.

Vietnam has two types of seasons—a hot, rainy season and a warm, dry season. During the wet season,

monsoon winds can bring rain almost every day. Sometimes heavy storms called typhoons hit the coast. A typhoon is like a hurricane with strong winds that causes flooding.

Ha Long Bay

Ha Long Bay lies off the northern coast of Vietnam. It is also known as the Bay of the Descending Dragon. Here almost three thousand small islands poke out of

Islands in Ha Long Bay

the water. Most of the islands are just large chunks of limestone. A few are large enough for people to live on. Visitors use small Vietnamese boats called **junks** to see the islands.

Junks on Ha Long Bay

Vietnam's thick rain forests provide shelter for many animals.

Thick rain forests and **mangrove** swamps cover parts of Vietnam. Elephants, tigers, black bears, and other large animals live in the forests. The forests also shelter smaller animals such as deer, hares, and many of the seven hundred different types of birds found in the country. However, some forests have been cut down to make room for farms. Many animals lose their homes when the forests are cleared.

A Land of Many People

About 79 million people live in Vietnam today. More people live in this country than live in California, Texas, and New York put together. Many Vietnamese families have **ancestors** that lived in the country thousands of years ago. Today, most of the people

Many Vietnamese people live along the coast.

live in small villages in the delta areas or along the coast.

Several different religions are practiced in Vietnam. One of the most popular is Buddhism, which spread from China and

Buddhists are worshipping inside a temple in Ho Chi Minh City.

India. People who worship Buddha pray in temples. Some other Vietnamese people practice Christianity. Catholic **missionaries** from France brought Christianity to Vietnam many years ago.

16

Many Vietnamese build small altars in their homes to remember their ancestors.

Most Vietnamese also worship the spirits of their ancestors. They build small altars in their homes and light candles to honor family members who have died. Families may also worship

Tho cong, or the God of Home, who protects the home and blesses the family.

Vietnam is a **Communist** state. The Vietnamese people get to elect some of their leaders, but not all of them. The people elect the members of the **legislature**. Then the legislature appoints the president of the country.

Struggles With Other Countries

Thousands of years ago, tribes of people moved south from China. They settled in the delta of the Red River. China controlled the northern region of Vietnam until 939. For the next eight hundred years, a series of **emperors** ruled the country.

France helped Vietnam build up towns in the 1800s.

Missionaries from France and other countries in Europe began visiting Vietnam in the late 1700s. In the 1880s, France took control of Vietnam. The French helped the people of Vietnam build new roads, railroads, and schools. But life for most Vietnamese was not easy. **Peasants** had to pay high taxes and rent to the French. They did not like the French ruling their country.

Many of the peasants in the north supported a new leader

Ho Chi Minh was the leader of the Communist party.

named Ho Chi Minh. Ho and his Communist Party fought the French and took over North Vietnam, which became its own country. The Vietnamese who did not like the Communists controlled South Vietnam.

Ho Chi Minh

Ho Chi Minh was Vietnam's most powerful leader. He formed the Vietnamese Communist Party and was president of North Vietnam from 1945 to 1969. Ho wanted his country to be free from control by other countries. He taught farmers to be soldiers. Then his army fought against the French and later the United States. Ho died during the Vietnam War. Later, the city of Saigon was renamed Ho Chi Minh City to honor this leader.

Ho Chi Minh's tomb is located in Hanoi.

War broke out between North and South Vietnam in 1957. As the war continued, the United States sent thousands of American soldiers to help South Vietnam fight against the North.

The war lasted a long time. Finally, the United States signed a peace treaty in 1973 and American soldiers left Vietnam. Two years later, the North Vietnamese took over the South. In 1976, the Socialist Republic of Vietnam was formed. Vietnam became one country again.

After the war, many South Vietnamese who had fought against the Communists were scared to live in their own

Many Vietnamese fled the country after the war.

country. Others found that their homes had been destroyed during the war and it was hard to earn a living. Almost one million South Vietnamese left Vietnam after the war. Some escaped to other countries by hiding in small boats. Many of these "boat people" live in the United States today.

The Economy

Even though Vietnam has several large cities, most people live in villages. Growing rice is a common way to earn a living. Farmers grow rice today in the same way their parents and grandparents did many years ago. Women and children plant the rice by hand. The men use water buffalo to

Two women are harvesting rice near Hanoi (above). A man is plowing his rice field (right).

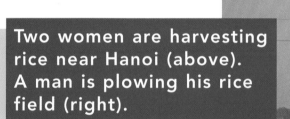

A boy casts his fishing net on the Mekong River.

pull the plows. Vietnamese farmers grow so much rice that they can sell some to other countries. Farmers also grow other crops such as sugarcane, corn, and peanuts. Some farmers raise pigs and cows.

Fishing is another big business in Vietnam. Fishermen cast large nets from their boats into the rivers to catch fish. Fishermen catch squid, crab, shrimp, and other types of fish to sell at the markets. Some farmers even raise fish in ponds near their homes.

Tourism is a new industry in Vietnam and brings millions of dollars into the country each year. There are many things to see and places to visit in the country. Young people visit Vietnam to enjoy the beaches. One popular spot is China Beach in Da Nang.

The Cuc Phuong Forest also draws tourists. It is a large rain forest south of Hanoi. It is one

The Cuc Phuong Forest is protected by the country.

The Thien Mu Pagoda is more than four hundred years old.

of the last pieces of protected forest in the country. Tourists find it difficult to walk through the forest because it is very rugged. Scientists find it is a great place to study wildlife.

Many old temples and **pagodas** (pa-GO-das) were destroyed in the war. Tourists visit the remains of these buildings. The Thien Mu Pagoda near the city of Hue still stands. An emperor had it built in 1601. It is seven stories high.

Vendors sell their goods at a busy market.

Most of Vietnam's roads and bridges were also destroyed during the war. Many have been rebuilt, but it is still hard to ship goods by truck. In the cities, motor scooters and **pedicabs** fill the narrow streets. Families travel by train or bus if they need to go long distances. People buy food and other goods at markets or from carts along the road.

Living in Vietnam Today

Life in Vietnam today includes traditions from many different countries. For example, Vietnamese is the official language, but some people also speak English or Chinese. They do not shake hands to greet one another as people in

Vietnamese children learn traditions from many cultures.

the United States do. Instead, they bow from the waist.

Rice and chopped vegetables are the main course for most family meals. Meat and fish may also be served.

A Vietnamese meal may include rice, vegetables, and meat.

Vietnamese cooks use lemongrass or other spices to flavor their food. They usually steam or fry the food in large pots called woks. A wok has a flat bottom and helps cook the food quickly. Many Vietnamese eat crusty French bread with their meals.

This is a tradition left from when France ruled Vietnam.

The Vietnamese celebrate holidays throughout the year. Many holidays are associated with the phases of the moon and the seasons. The biggest celebration of the year is Tet,

People celebrate Tet at a festival in Hanoi.

which celebrates the Vietnamese New Year. It is a happy festival in which fireworks are set off. The New Year does not fall on the same day each year, but it is always in late January or early February.

Families clean and paint their homes before Tet begins. No one wants to sweep during the celebration. They might sweep away their good luck. Families eat special food such as sweet rice cakes. Some people cut watermelons during New Year.

The darker red the melon is, the better their luck will be for the year!

A watermelon with a dark red center means good luck for the year.

To Find Out More

Here are some additional resources to help you learn more about Vietnam.

 **Books**

Dooley, Norah. **Everybody Cooks Rice.** Minneapolis: CarolRhoda Books, 1991.

Gibbons, Alan. **The Jaws of the Dragon.** Minneapolis: Lerner Publications, 1994.

Huynh Quang Nhuong. **Water Buffalo Days: Growing Up in Vietnam.** New York: HarperCollins, 1997.

Moehn, Heather. **World Holidays: A Watts Guide for Children.** Danbury, CT: Franklin Watts, 2000.

Organizations and Online Sites

Embassy of Vietnam
1233 20th Street NW,
Suite 400
Washington, DC   20036
*http//www.vietnam
embassy-usa.org*

The embassy can give you information about Vietnam's government, culture, geography, and history.

Ha Long Bay, The World Heritage Site
*http//www.halongbay.
halong.net.vn*

See pictures and read the legends about the limestone islands in Ha Long Bay.

North Vietnam Lowland Rain Forests
*http://www.nationalgeographic.
com/wildworld/profiles/
terrestrial/im/im0141.html*

This site contains interesting facts about Vietnam's rain forests.

Vietnam
*http://www.asianinfo.org/
asianinfo/vietnam/
aboutvietnam.htm*

You can find information about wildlife, religion, history, and more at this site.

Vietnam Online: The American Experience
*http://www.pbs.org/wgbh/
amex/vietnam/*

This site has information about the United States's involvement in the Vietnam War.

Important Words

ancestor a family member from an earlier generation, such as a great-grandfather

Communism a belief that a community, not individual people, should own land and resources

delta a deposit of soil formed near the mouth of a river

emperor a ruler of a large area of land

junk a flat-bottomed boat with high sails

legislature an elected group of people given the power to make laws

mangroves trees or shrubs that grow in shallow salt water

missionary someone sent to do religious work in another country

pagoda a tower-shaped Buddhist temple

peasant a farmer or worker

pedicab a small vehicle with pedals, three wheels, and a roof that carries passengers

Index

Meet the Author

Shirley Wimbish Gray, MA, has been a writer and educator for more than twenty years. In addition to writing children's books, she coordinates cancer education at the University of Arkansas for Medical Sciences. She also consults with scientists and doctors about their writing. She lives in Little Rock, Arkansas, with her husband and two sons.